I0111332

Abyss in Remission
My Dance with Pancreatic
Cancer Recovery
and other poems

by
William Armstrong

Front cover image:
Turner, Joseph Mallard William (1775-1851)
Fishermen at Sea. Exhibited 1796. Oil on canvas, 91.4x122.2 cm.
Photo Credit: Tate, London / Art Resource NY

© William Armstrong   armstrong40510@yahoo.com

Disclaimer: Please read before continuing.

If you know someone who's ill,
With any form of cancer,
Do not assume they suffer as I did,
Ask them and let them answer.

Talking is something that clears all concerns,
Compare theirs with mine, if you must,
You'll learn they're tough, much to respect,
But, their travail probably isn't as rough.

With that being said,
Please read ahead.

William Armstrong

This book is affectionately
dedicated to my parents,
Lew and Jane Armstrong,
for all their care and help.

And, to Doctor Dilip
Parekh and my surgical
staff at Huntington hospital
in Pasadena, for enabling
me to be here today.

ABYSS IN REMISSION
My Dance with Pancreatic
Cancer Recovery

PART ONE:
The Descent

CANTO I– It Begins

A year like most, seeing
Sky, mountain,
The dark of my closed
Eyelids,
Still meeting and tasting

Cool
Lightness,
Windy delicious, a gift of
Spring,
All soon to change,

Sledgehammer.
March, a lamb, "Let there
Be more rain."
I plead to no-one. Unheard,
My cry,

Facing an oven of
Desiccation. Flowers,
Trees, grass, me all deflate,
Evaporate.
A sucking dry, ill manner.

A kiss of "bye, you old
You."
No alarm bells
Clanging yet. I'm daisy
Yellow, hemolytic jaune,

Jaundice
Tawny, piss backing up,
Jacking up
My deep sleep. Death
Knight bearing a

Golden banner.
Cork my sick. Finding the
Reason,
Lasts a season, missing out
On

Fountain brook, a
Mountain of look,
Too few eyes to detect the
Infection.
Or, maybe, too many

Guests trespass the manor.
Ants from this jaune, not

Mounded
And building, they bit,
Tore and I

Tore to soothe the troops
And yell "Calm,
You burn." My mounds
From scratching
Grew and built and red

Wept
Bleeding and bleating my
Pain.
Some say they are medals
Hard- fought won,

From my joust spar with a
Dragon.
Nothing so grand won, my
Grand ones. Only
My stand firm to stay

Seeing a
Life, even my swelled,
Crimson blue-black life, to
Be
Embraced by

Touch, smell, see, hear.
Everyone the when, to
Abiding embrace my
Saving, blind bliss,
Ignorance. The cause of

My aching was not yet
Known or named.
I am too low upstairs to
Know I should
Cry and tremble. Still

Scanning brave
Past the lava-gutted food
Rejection,
To name the color of the
Zephic breeze,

The flavor of my most
Soul-saving painter,
The electric bass thud
Touch reverberating
Through my car, through

Me,
Pounding passing
Every mile of my drive to
Job and home with fervent
Feel beating. Never

Too sick to earn green
And Gold. Rent never
Stops. My grateful
'Thanks' and respectful
Heart-touch to my

Hippocratic
Lords, those people of the

Purple, Royal astute
Sawbones for that.
Too soon. I must measure

Out my hurricane head-
Long plunge. I must
Confess my
Victory in order proper to
My battle.

And so, a year unlike most.
March first,
April second, May third,
June
Fourth.

Eureka! Pin-cushioning
Done! Sherlock
Searching done! Probing,
Prodding, Pushing,
Over! Blooding, bleeding,

IV feeding, hating
Waiting, hurry, wait, could
Be gone, hurry, wait,
Moving on, hurry, wait,
Must

Be quick, hurry
Wait, stop, start, cheeks
Apart, too cold in here,
Have a heart, hurry, wait, a
Room that's new; here's a

Broom- away you blue.
Hurry, wait, no gloom,
That's you, take this cup,
Please go pee, hurry, wait,
Back to me!

Too loud, I know. I know.
This is book one, the
Descent of a man, and
The fight where he stood
Old school, a knight

Bounden by ethics to live
And
Survive and
Stride the other side of
Pain. "You don't

Quit or cry. You don't quit
Or
Cry. You
Don't quit or cry." I was
Told. And listened; sold

The notion by old Roman
Emperors and older Vedic
Sages And new children
Giving off their
Energy of "keep walking,

And breathing and
laughing
And loving, because it is

Worth it!"
Don't leave me, my gilded,

Glowing hearts, and we
Will see
If it is. Calm, come, and be
Hearty and
Heartened and hardened in

Aspect of strength. Grasp
Your diamond, shining
Shields and your defenses
Gird for me, and thee,
For this comes next is

Tough and tawdry
And tender. Watch and
Listen as I
Tread and whisper and roar
Through hell.

CANTO II- My Healers, All

You listen to us, you
Healers of hearts' souls,
With minds
That wrap our pain, that
Knife edge, that winter

Chill, in the warmth of
Meet
My sister,
Meet my brother, meet me
Strength, and leave

Us whole and sound and
Sane to ears that
Aren't ears or heart or
Brain, but simply disease. I
Speak, of course, of the

Uppercase 'C'; that rolling
Bounding ocean of
Directionless power
That
Touches us all, even those

Furthest from its
Devastating shore, who can
But stand and watch,
Helpless, as the ships
Of our bodies are pounded

Upon the ever-present
Surface of its never-
Pleasant swells. A cruise
Ship with room service of
The worst sort;

Which passage costs but
The coin of
Mindless, midnight-black
Ill-luck.
You saviors listen, lifting,

Holding, broad-
Shouldering,
Patient explaining,
Patiently
Braining our plight,

Far sight, from prior
Wound, our courage
Swooned,
Just hold us, must mold us
From wandering faint,

Shivering, quivering, to
'quiescing saint, facing the
Squad,
Firing a volley of our own
At our disease; our unease.

My Hippocratic lords and
Ladies, giants in our
Planet's

Plight, re-makers, re-
Fitters,

Doctors, nurses, bathers,
Testers, dispensers,
Feeders, bleeders,
Encouragers, up lifters,
Explainers, trainers, EMTs,

Administrators,
Researches, relievers,
Believers that
You and we will certain
Prevail. Then, to your

Hearth,
My hearts, to home with
You,
To follow your marathon
Days with family, fine

Homage, they, the next
Generation, veneration, of
Seeking, questing, illness-
Besting
Busting text books to next

Defeat the fearsome
Knight-slayer plaque. The
Morn's new fixers and
Finders
And severed-cell binders.

Tomorrow's broad
Shouldered
Atlas. Understand, my
Dears, my hearts, you
Lords and ladies, I speak

My music, from a different
All-time.
I speak, just now, the
Beginning of the
Fight, years ago, when you

Found me and bound
Me and sounded me out
With "It's going to get
Rough."

CANTO III- As Orpheus Trekked, Do I

I awoke to tubes and foggy
Eyes,
A room of beige, white
Angles,
Glass all one wall, half-

Way
Up for watching
My supine repose. Those
Many machines were
Monitored

As they monitor my beats
And lub-dubs. I'm all eyes
And
Sight and seeing. Some
Small hearing, also, as

There
Is little to hear; droning,
Buzzing, shuffling. Arms
And
Legs move on command,

But barely, and warily and
Why?
The bars of my bed bring
Rarely any reason or
Rhyme

For
Climbing their sides to
Escape. I don't want to
Leave; the bed, the care,
The solid knowledge they

Know my plight and are
Warring with wanton
Death-
Cells spreading carelessly,
Quickly, coldly, soundly

Bringing
Me roundly within sight of
The scythe-swinging
Life-severer, that endless
Fiend and foe, who

Beckons
'Let's go' to its mansion of
Darkest night, final
Night, where all who visit
Are welcomed with a

Whispering roar, then gone
Goodbye, and I, myself am
Not yet ready to join that
Twerp in ushering out
Of sight my life. I'm not

Ready to go. There is too
Much
To see, hear, taste, sensate.

And, neither, too, do my
Lords and ladies who cut

And swab and inject and
Inspect and hold their oath
So
Close they
Can't but call on all

They've known and know
To
Quick forestall my falling
And calling out from in
My mind and heart and all

I
Have to them to
Save my life. And, answer
My call, they do and true
And wick a light to golden-

White
Search the why and
Wherefore
Of my wasting life eraser.
But, trust me,

My gilded, golden hearts,
The manner of their saving
Hurts.
It stings and
Sticks and burns and tears

My night of sleep apart, by
Hourly pokes to check my
Cringing and craven blood
For
Sugar level and

White count mean and
Emergence of a clotted
Flow
Within the alleys of hemo
Streams. And, all this time,

Believe or not, as you will,
Despite the words of
Wailing this moment
Spoken, I did have the use
And made the

Use of pain-killing, shock-
Stilling drugs.
They were Dilaudid,
Morphine, Vicodin and
Codeine;

All dosed to make my pain
A
Dream. Satin drugs, velvet
Hugs within my blood and
Brain, to halt the uptake

Receptors' work and keep
Me close within the frame
Of human thought so I can

Explain how I feel, if I
Feel,

And on a scale of one to
Ten, how extreme. I didn't
Know
Yet how much these meds
Worked their magic

Threads.
These opioid treats,
Deadening sweets- until
They took
Me off them.

CANTO IV- My Intake

But, that's not yet. I won't
Get
Ahead of my tale. We now
Should speak, talk, as it
Were, of diet, or none, for

None there was. For four
Long weeks I did drink
And eat through tubes; an
I.v. of saline and liquid fat
And

TPN, ingredients concoct
Of
All things good except
Bulk and taste satisfaction.
No complaint I'm giving,

I promise you that, they
Worked their wondrous
Sustaining invasion to let
Me life maintain and well.
But, speaking as one who

Fed with ardor, reveling in
The
Banquet of lush, thick,
Sweet,
Sour, tough, tender,

Cheesy, meaty, gravy-
Laden, salted haven of
Sharp and mild,
Gourmet-styled filling,
Thrilling, stuff-your-face-

At-a furious-
Pace, syrup-drenched,
Pepper-stenched, butter-
Dripping,
Chewing, tearing all the

Meals before this time of
Food divine which made
Me weigh three hundred
And twenty
Gorged, sated, over-

Weighted pounds; to this
One who
Ate and loved what I ate,
To this one, me, a bag on a
Tube

Is truly inadequate food. I
Will say this, you give me
Leave, that goop in a bag
Smelled like roast beef. I
Kid you not, hallucinate

Perhaps, but a tube-meal
Smelled
Like sweet roast beef.

And, what of drink, there
Was none, enough to wet

My
Lips and tongue; that's all.
And worse than no food
To love, was the loss of
Any fresh cooling cove, to

Dive into; bathing my body
Fresh with cold, clean,
Clear and crystalline aqua.
My tongue, it swelled; no
Rain in hell, no fountains

Nor mountain brooks
Lined with sheltering tree-
Leaning wet banks where I
Could shout my thanks for
Drinking until I laved

All sweet and wet and
More to get of clear, blue
Relief from my dry, hot
Crumpling body begging
For one

Mere gulp, even luke-
Warm PLEASE! "No, not
Yet.
We have to see if you are
Clear of scarring, stopping,

Blockage met with blood
And bile that cannot get
From out your torso to
Shed
Your waste, so

Not a drop or morsel you
Taste, until we're sure
It's safe, my patient, be
Patient and you'll
Have to wait."

CANTO V- My Plague, My Own

And, so. What sort of
Sickly-sour, killing, dour,
Unwanted power beat my
Breast and got the best of
Me? By what name was

My
Death- dredging
Be-clawed, be-fanged,
Flame-scaled, fear-winged
Beast known? What was

My endemic illness?
Think you of that pipe-
Playing, cloven-hoofed
Reveler PAN. Think, now,
He plays and

Pipes and dances in the
Attic
Of his garden palace. His
Attic. Pan's Attic. You are
Not far from

Naming the beast.
PANCREATIC is the 'C' I
Swam, the ocean tide of
Neoplasm which crashed
Over my drowning form

And filled my torso with a
Mortal froth and had me
Spluttering in red,
Wet guttering like a candle
Half blown out by a

Freezing gale. My gentle
'C', creeping 'C', silent
Adenocarcinoma, my
Illness passing deft and
Competent among the frail

Tissuing miracles, issuing
Ventricles waging their
Whispering war against
Neuroendocrine blight
Crawling to end my

Existence;
This pancreatic 'C' was the
Thundering footfall which
Yearly strides the
Organelles with hammer

Falls of
Tumescent, bulging, soft,
Spongy grunge, sludging
Its creeping epidemic
Terror across every

Continent of this once-in-
An-eternity breathing,

Blue-green haven and
Home.
Pancreatic pandemic. A

Plague blacker than the
Black plague blight of our
European middle ages of
Rat infested
Killing rot. Pancreatic

Carcinoma. Its first touch
Is most always in a life's
Middle-age, but rarely
Spied out until the Autumn
Of our

Years, that time of spring-
Gone summer, house just
Getting broken-in, family
Just getting broken-in,
Passing the years of

'nothing else matters
'cept me and us.' leaving
Little for fear and hope and
Pain and regret to yell
Except "TOO LATE!"

And by that time, in the
Shaded, dusk
Half- light of Sun's three-
Quarter set into children all
Grown, small beating

Hearts of their own, job's
Complete, just rest my feet
And sit my
Seat in a well-worn chair,
Silver hair, job well done-

Just
Then does it come, for
Some, to remind us
'Human, you're new men
and women'

Because time and the
Pendulum back-and forth-
Us
To face our mortality from
This roll-of-the-dice place

Among the footprints of
Prince and princess, which
We all are, everyone of us,
And who would want to
Live forever anyway? I for
One.

PART TWO:
The Trek

CANTO VI- How Does It Feel?

Of all the questions about
My health, "How do you
Feel?" is number one.
Then, second on the list of
'How' is "How did it feel,

Your life
Of fun among the fumes
And flames of that terrain
Of tearing pain, your daily
Trek in that domain that

Myth has termed Lord
Hade's plain?"
But first, before
Descriptions flow, and you
Know my chronic woe,

Please, you permit my lack
Of wit describing pain in
Terms
Profane to that place
Below. Anything that does

Distract from what is grand
About our time upon this
Living, breathing tract of

Self-Sustaining Earth
sublime, I term an onerous

And evil pact. There is no
Heaven nor a hell. It makes
My story an easy tell.
They're allegories,
What's good, what's not,

What's easy and light,
What's highly wrought.
And, my opinion, just my
Thought, any pain that
Makes reflection

Travail on any other focal
Point, which makes us too
Vigorous introspect, is
Malevolent and fraught
With diminished poise. I

Was
Already well acquainted
With how over-worked our
Nerves can get, from days
In youth spent nursing

Wounds sustained from
That source
And this. Some say these
Early poundings founded
Within me a much stiller

Pillar, so to speak, of
Support in my weak and
Green days,
My tender times, for later
Ham-handed slamming and

Instilling, as I tip-toed shy
Of my mother's warmth, a
Sort of 'oak-in-the-wind'
Ability
To bend but not topple,

Losing only some of my
Bark to lovers' carved life
Initials of scalpel and
Drain. These first and
Foremost knocks and

Rocks were meant by life
To leave me breathing
Without weaving too wide
A path of dazed and hazy
Meanderings. So, when the

Time arrived,
September of an already
Tenaciously audacious
Year, which saw me
Running from jaundice

Disappeared follow-up
Meets, to x-ray exams to

explain to me the presence
Of a centimeter huge mass,
Clinging like moss, closing

My bile duct, that needed
Duct tucked within my
Battered torso, used to
Conduct the noxious,
Green-black vile cellular

Leftover soup, turgid goop,
Those salty, screaming,
Itchy atoms
Combined to turn me from
Pink and calm to yellow

And yelling. Imagine every
Itch you ever felt, babe
Days 'til now, all at once,
Tickling and
Tingling you from dawn to

Dawn, in a dismal dance of
Burning and blooming and
Not enough hands to
Scratch them all and
Everywhere.

Scratching and digging and
Tearing until scratched and
Bloody and torn, with scars
Discolored dark and
Showing still today. Some

Meds made
The maddening matter a
Lesser disaster, but not
With the loose and watery
Bathroom leavings and

Profuse, nauseous, gut-
Knocking
Retching and wretched
Dehydration, which only
Worsened my feeble,

Confused body battering
By a scourge of blood-
Pressure
Peaks and valleys, flogging
My physique with heated

Sleep and sweaty nesting,
Still attempting to keep my
Living space spruced and
Clean, and
All from the comforting,

Soft and safe haven of bed.
I must admit, in this, I
Failed. And, through these
First months, because, yes,
This lasted

Months, was the assailant
Headache, sitting on my

Forehead like some unseen
Vulture, pecking deep and
Moving spider-like and

Mammoth-heavy, back and
Forth across my skull
Muscle sheath, so I never
Had the opportunity to
Ignore it. After months, the

Disease was
Found, coursing 'round
And removed very smooth.
Nine hours on a table I
Never got to see, and

Waking up to parents I
Barely knew, in ICU,
Thinking thickly and
Speaking a salad of phrases
Met with smiles for their

Incoherence. I remember
The room was robust with
A frigid expanse of
Cold air and colder
Personalities, going about

Their wonderful business
Of welcoming me
Brusquely back to the land
Of the living.
Still no word of what

Burden bedeviled me.
Until this time, I wandered
Walking-dead, where I was
Told what to do and where
To go and whom to

See, not knowing the
Proper questions to ask.
So, wall after pliant wall of
Question marks I sped
Lazily into, my car a carnal

Wreck,
Accelerating from zero to
Nothing in seven months.
March of my melancholic
Year was yellow,

Extravagant misery
Incarnate, stretching
To September, better but
Worse, post Whipple
Surgery. Idle. Slow.

Inactive. Sluggish.
Slothful. Lazy. Could run a
Decent mile
Before my decline.
Suddenly, can't walk for

Two minutes without a
Rest, every step an

Exercise in light-headed
Vertigo. My very own
Roller-

Coaster of roiling,
Plunging, climbing
Clumsiness. Could pump a
Hundred push-ups no
Sweat. Suddenly, a

Radiating, flabby pain in
Sloppy arms
And legs that howl with
The herculean effort of
Lifting a cell phone or

Newspaper. Then, they
Wheel in a wheel chair,
That rolling, loathsome
Set-in-stone that I'm sick
And needful of mechanical

Support. An erstwhile
Android; a frightened
Frankenstein, knit and
Stitched and grunting out
My replies to questions I

Rarely understood. One
Silver lining in this time of
My slaughter- a nurse with
A sponge and
Some water. It availed me

Nothing within the realm
Of depraved fantasy, but,
Still a quick and dear
Memory to offset the clear
And distinct

Knowledge that I was
Unable to care for my
Basic needs. And, through
This all, was the incessant
And ever-present ache,

Glowing red-black in
My stomach, besotted with
Unreduced enzymes and
Undiluted acid; a
Ballooning bowling ball of

Pressure that pinned my
Attention to the
Stern harshness of the
Aching persistence that
Reared its volcanic,

Branding, thudding
Insistence once the
Dilaudid and morphine
Ended. My
Torso still wails and

Whines, to this day. An
Acid reducer is my pain

Refuser. And, a virus is
Quicker caught than
Previous to my changed

State
Of health.
While still stilling under
The warm comforter of my
Awesome opiates, thinking

Was a slinking process.
Minor actions required
Major
Preparation and
Instruction. Favorite

Pastimes past took a
Monumental declination
And reduction. Always a
Ready reader, eager to
Devour pages

By the hour, I stared
Instead at the grassy
Landscape and rosy bushes
Outside my sliding door,
And found a profound

Indolence
Preferable to engaging my
Medicated and menial
Mind in the empty, endless
Chatter that the printed

Page had become. Solemn
Staring at
Eternity's oblivion in a
Single flower blossom
Became my all, my

Everything, my nothing.
Yet, no part of my pain-
Free, thought-free,
Individual-less brain cried
Or cried 'stop!' Where is

The fortitude to fight or
Flight when might is taken
In an exchange of an
Absence of
Agony? Whither went my

Wherewithal to argue in
The face of a void of
Misery? In a glad
Acceptance of comfort and
Momentary peace, the

Eye of my soon-to-be
Hurricane of torment. Do I
Exaggerate? Am I being
Overly melodramatic? We
Shall see.

CANTO VII- After ICU

Post-ICU were weeks of
Working at walking, weak-
Willed and waning. My
Weight dropped drastically
To one hundred and sixty

Soft and skeletal
Pounds. I saw the true bone
Structure of my middle-
Aged face, for the first
Time since high school.

My eyes had sunk
Shockingly into their
Sockets, leaving me
Looking in constant wide-
Eyed daze at everything

And everyone. But, there
Was no wonder in my
Mind. Nor any humor,
Resentment, happiness,
Sorrow, shame, merriment,

Desire, terror, or any
Thought processing we
Average happy humans
Take for granted. My
Trudging, stoop-

Shouldered, shambling
Body mirrored my mind.
A room in a crowded,
Dowdy after-care facility
Met my

Needs. The first of many
Inclement incidents to
Indicate a rough ride in the
Offing was, while resting
On a hot evening, people-

Watching
As I was watched and
Matched, pain-for-pain, by
My neighboring, wayward
Dazed and hazy neighbor,

Started when a flush of
Frigid
Heat shook me, centering
On my already cantering
Stomach. I leaned over the

Bed edge and deposited a
Pretty pint of tar-black,
Thick,
Sticky sick on the
Linoleum. Cleaned up,

Both me and the floor, and
Pounded soundly

By elevated blood-
Pressure, I turned, leaned
And heaved

Again. The facility's head-
Doctor sauntered in and
Pronounced me in need of
Another trip, via
Screaming, sirened

Limousine, back to an
Emergency room. Eight
Hours in a room the size of
My current closet, trying,
And

Flopping, to make pleasant
Small-talk with my ever-
Patient parents. Then, seen
And screened and
Pronounced infected by an

I.V. picline.
Leaving on yet another
Gurney, my whipple
Surgeon,
Mindful of my mending,

Assured me it would be
Hastily and dandily
Handled
And, by the way, casually
Mentioned I also had

Pneumonia! The medicine
He proscribed for my fluid-
Logged, virus-veined lungs
Smelled of rotten eggs.
Back to after-care. But, a

Privileged patient I had
Become, with only a single
Room-mate, and a quiet,
Comfortable one. Stroke
Had his system, so we

Made the perfect pair,
Neither of us able to speak
Much or think with
Complex effect. Social
Disconnect was our

Burdensome bond. Days
Seeing only sun and sky
Seemed our all.
Then, there were the
Nights. No horror movie or

Terror torn television show
Equaled
The immersive, macabre
Sounds echoing through
The

Dimly lit halls in a
Building where one quarter

Of the humans are
Mending various
Hurts, and three quarters

Are fraught with frightened
And
Frightening mental
Impairments. We were, all
Of us, well cared for and

Clean.
But, it can't be denied,
Some existed in corridors
More damp and dark than
I.

Once, wandering in a rare
Instance of standing ability
And walking agility, I
Shuffled in search of who-
Knows-what, and of a

Certain
Heard a baby's cry. Ever
The mis-guided hero, I
Searched
And beseeched a nurse to

Help the babe, whereupon
I was told, calmly and
Caringly,
There were no babies in
The building. It became

Apparent to me, my mind
Was
Melting and my
Personality, always touting
Traits of some common

Sense and
Sensibility, was warping.
Put to bed and medded to
Sleep, I
Awoke to a worse

Nightmare.
An ambulance took me to
Another hallway of
Agonized anticipation
Where I was pain-pillowed

And reclined in
A second hallway. Then a
Room of beeping machines
And tables laden with
Instruments of saving

Torture. One of my
Hippocratic lords
Came in to poke in a
Needle,
Amazed at my vein's

Reaction. A rare
Phenomenon, he explained

Bemused, in patients
Pounded long-term,
The sought after vein

Flattened
Itself, in a cowardly
Response of sub-conscious
Escape. I could readily
Believe it. Finally found,

Another vein
Was needled. Ten minutes
Later, my hero of healing
Produced another needle, a
Movie prop from every

Danger fraught film of
Ripping
Damage ever made. The
Doctor explained that a
Five-and-a-half inch long

Needle was needed to
Reach and draw off
Abscessed fluid,
Collecting in lakes of
Serum

Throughout my torso. It
Wouldn't take long, so no
Need to mallet me
Unconscious. The needle
Went in, pain killers pitiful

To
Its plunge, and removed a
Liter of red, viscous fluid.
Needle out, then back in.
Another liter. Experience

Finished. Oh, and the
Pneumonia had returned.
Just sayin'.
Sitting in wait for my ride
Back in the back of my

After-burning ambulance,
A candy-
Striper, one of those
Wonderful volunteers of
Cheer, brought a small dog

To me for comfort and
Doggy distraction. My
Poodle hero.
Racing too slowly in return
To my room, the meds to

Pain-free me wore off.
Doubled over, feeling
Alive, dammit, I called for
Dilaudid. Ten
Minutes later, lying

Gratefully in television-
Addled relief, I drifted off

To dreamless sleep. I
Would see another needle
Of five-and-a-half inch

Horror a
Week later.
"Here's breakfast." "I
Can't." "Here's lunch." "I
Can't." "Here's dinner." "I

Can't." "Please sit up." "I
Can't."
"Just for two minutes." "I
Can't" "Let's walk." 'I
Can't."

"Every other day." "I
Can't." Let's go outside."
"I can't." "Read a book."
"I can't."
Six weeks of "I can't",

During which my long,
Lazy days of lassitude
Were broken by trips to fix
Liquid pouring from a
Torso-staple removed

Closing
A fluid-filled abscess,
Collected in a colostomy
Crud catcher, followed by
A pig-tail drain on the

Opposite side of the battle-
Field of my torso. I
Had begun to eat in tiny
Amounts. This was halted
For another hateful week.

Then, news of the world,
Brought on a golden cloud
Of
Dolorous celebration! I
Was leaving to the palace

Of my parents! Life would
Be a
Return of quick recovery
And of warm and delicious
Holidays, right?

Not exactly.

CANTO VIII- The Palace of My Parents

Mid-October. That time of
Calm, cool autumn breezes
And festival fun, of warm,
Gentle nights and
Temperate days, leisurely

Laziness,
Leading to year's end.
Mid-October I was
Released from hospital
After-care into the familiar,

Familial embrace of my
Waiting parents. Once
Again, as in my suckling
Youth, I looked to those
Who had raised and reared

Me for solace. And, they
Answered my cry.
Breathing easier,
Feeling freer, I sat in the
Back seat of my carriage of

Rescue, my parent's gold-
Colored, golden chariot; an
SUV with over a decade's
Traverse in
Miles, now performing,

With horses loping under
Its hood, smooth and sleek,
Hooves rubber, an
Extrication, a liberation;
My discharge from

A castle of serious,
Focused, mindful, human
And humane salvation, to
Their three room palace of
Light and life and familiar,

Friendly funny talk
And tip-toeing. My stately
Stay on quilted comfort.
Roaming, unsteady, among
Curio memories, small

Treasures to be asked
About,
Realizing my parents are
More mystery to me than I
Thought. Time's gaping

Gap, of my own self-
Centered work and play,
Had left a rift, a black-
Hole heft, of ignorance of
All that they had done and

Seen and acquired. Each
Treasure holds a story,

Charming me with the
Hearing, they highly
Pleased with the telling.

This manse of safe recoup
And couches covered in
Plush delight and
Miserable me, would, for
Ten shuffling,

Waning, wandering weeks,
Be my home and haven.
Days following my parole
From after-care
Observation were a

Cacophony of relief,
Hunger, denial, exhaustion
And sleepy wakefulness,
All
Heightened by the growing

Withdrawal, sweaty,
Confusing, itchy (again),
From the dilaudid and
Morphine. Cold-turkey
Was my main

Meal from the deadening
Duo. Vicodin, vice of my
New pleasure, took their
Place. Vicodin, ill-
Equipped to please, sat

Stone-heavy and
Burning in my stomach,
The main ingredient in a
Savage cocktail of stomach
Acid, nature's enzymes,

Chemical enzymes (Creon)
And acid
Reducers (ineffective), all
Arguing pitifully for
Attention in a stomach that

Had shrunk in starvation.
Turning to television, that
Wonderful,
Vapid vacation from
Thought, provided some

Distraction, as long as my
Body movement was
Minimal and marginal.
Sunlight through a wall
Length window, bright in

Its bitter-sweet blaze,
Reminding me all was not
Lost, seemed to me to say
"Your world is still turning
'round me and

you with it". Heartening
Sol star. Eons seen,

Worshipped, cursed, care-
Free everyone's
Everything. My burden

Seemed light compared to
Our life-sustaining sol star,
The sun.
Out of bed to try to eat and
Keep it down. My stomach

Crying 'NO!'. My
Nutritional needs and past
Eating habits crying "YES!
Put me back at
The endless banquet table

Where I wore a bib of all-
You-can-eat." No such
luck. A cup of sweet,
tangy, Sticky pudding, and
I visit The

Bathroom twice to bring it
Up. Fear and despair begin
Reaching past the receding
Effects of the opiate duo,
To spike my chest with a

Pair of
Hairy, tearing talons. Fear
At nothing in particular,
Just a dead-pan dread, part
Chemical, part comical in

Its unfamiliarity to my
Light,
Supportive surroundings,
And despair, topping the
Rise of my awakening

Realization, my coming of
Clarity, that all is out of
Anyone else's hands
But my own. That, soon,
The palace of my parents

Would give way to my tiny
Apartment where, always
Proud to live alone, strong
In
My independence, I faced

A debilitated state and fate
Of worrisome wandering
And doing for myself,
Always pleasant to think
On before, but frightening

And forthcoming.
My father, always an
Excellent provider, but
Admitting to being less
Adapted to the more

Emotional understanding
Of

My protracted plight,
Always stood ready to lend
A hand when necessary.

My mother, more
Equipped, from her own
Health frailties and
Insistent
Issues, offered advice and

Sage suggestions for
Lessening the amount of
Awful impact. Day trips to
Dreamscapes near water or
Desert scenery increased

My morale, sunk to almost
Nothing by this time. A
Picture, taken of me during
One of these pleasing
Scene

Parades, shook me with its
Depiction of the dire
Disaster I had become. I
Gazed in dismay at a man
Gaunt and stooped, skin

Stretched
Loosely over a sagging
Skeleton, looking a century
Older than I was, and
Feeling much the same.

But, despite this, I did
Begin to rebuild,
Day by dreary day, to my
Former and present self.
But, my reconstruction was

Ponderous. Ten weeks of
Trying to ignore, and
Failing
To do so, the reality
Rocking and thunderously

Silent shift in my tiny
World, was burned,
Branding-iron, into my
Memory, and will stay
There for life, as will my

Parents' part in easing this
Event.
January second. The long
Drive home, hopeful that,
Once again in command of

My life, I would begin to
See a clear vision of a
Crystal
Future, where my haunted
Trek through Hade's

Hollows and hallowed
Ground, would see a cease
And be an ease back to me.

But, it was not to be.

CANTO IX- Life's Food Orgy

<u>Before the Whipple surgery</u>

Pizza- toasty, dry, salty
Crust crunching flour
Dusted. Thickly running
Lava-like butter-soft
Cheese. Tangy, lightly

Seared toppings of
Greasy pepperoni and
Sharply sweet sausage.
Prime Rib- fatty slab of
Moist, dripping mallet-

Pounded, peppered\salted
Tooth-sinking
Perfection. A side salad of
Cool, light, colorful
Dressing dressed delight.

Sips of fruit-toned, tannin
Tasting cabernet.
Enchiladas- spicy
Hot, bitter chili pudding
Cheese puddles melting,

Mixing with gooey,
Flawless refried

Excellence. Grilled fish-
Baked, breaded thick
Brick of lemon-drizzled,

Tart tasting trout, sliding
Into a side salad singing
Sweetly with vinaigrette
Tang. Washed down with
Pear toned,

Popping chardonnay.
Orange chicken- tangy
Tangerine, dripping honey-
Thick filling chicken.
Nuggets larded and grilled

Of ground-up
Greatness resting, waiting
Bedded on soft, sodium-
Rich rice. Tear legs of
Drooping beaded drops

Down a glass of clear ice
Water. Steak and
Eggs- charred to a well-
Done dish, cooked cow
Muscle made a maddening

Meat addict's favorite
Breakfast, fast-breaking
Fatted, eye-
Watering, chewy
Gastronomical

Awesomeness, side-by-
Tantalizing-side with over-
Easy globs of salted and
peppered, butter-greased
Eggs, sopped up with

Triangles of sweet
Strawberry jam smeared
Sourdough bread. Sushi-
Fish, always a favorite
Dish, raw, sweet sea

Samples, rice-rolled in a
Jacket of jade-green
Seaweed, blasting taste
Buds beautifully, dotted
With a ginger garnish

Gathering
Gloriously in a blending of
All that satisfies and sates.
Appetite aptly appeased.
French toast- egg-soaked,

Butter-laden, grilled bread,
Powder sugar sprinkled,
Drenched in thick, superb
Syrup, any flavor, eggs and
Sausage and bacon besides,

Laving my tongue in life's
Luscious flavor orgy,
Breakfast, lunch or dinner.

After the Whipple surgery

The first four fetid years
Following my cancer
Removal repose, eating
Was the exact opposite of
All that. Enough said.

CANTO X- My Body's Desolation

I've written, in extent, of
The ruin, the destruction,
Physiologically speaking,
In terms tough and honest
And humorless, that my

Tender
And vulnerable, shredded
Torso experienced, hoping
To brave the remembering,
Onto word-processed

Canvas; a true, terrible
Depiction of
Slow desperation and ugly,
Raw, swollen pain. But,
Things can always be

Worse. Timing back to
Post-jaundice, after-itchy,
Yellowed joy, my
Delirium was heightened
By a lessening of white

Cells and blood volume.
Anemia, that scourge of
Vampires throughout
Literature, had
Begun to color my body

With an absence of color.
My alarms began
Claxoning when the ends
Of my normally red-pink
Fingers and toes began

To lighten towards
Translucence. Then,
Spreading, my pallid skin
Wrinkled with the
Accompanying dryness.

Rooms, which otherwise
Radiated a soothing,
Comfortable blanket of
Healthy heat, were turned
Ice-box chilly. Climbing

Stairs
Became climbing Mount
Everest, without sufficient
Blood to transport omni-
Present oxygen throughout

My gasping limbs and
Organs.
Dropping blood pressure
Headaches blurred my
Vision. All this while

Leaving cups of blood with
Every bathroom sit-down.
But, more about
That in another canto in
This poem. With anemia

Comes a decreased ability
To mend, as a star fades
And extinguishes with
Insufficient fire at its
Core. As my drained and

Draining body struggled,
The strain showed in
Bizarre and minute details.
My fingernails curled and
Shriveled. My calves, feet

And especially my toes,
Screamed with muscle
Contractions, like the limbs
Of a frightened turtle,
Slowly gripping in

Painful spasm. Knots of
Tension, which traveled by
Endocrine elevator, from
My feet-basement to my
Skull-attic, made sleep a

Sought
After luxury. On the day I
Left after care for the

Palace of my parents, three
I.v. tubes were removed

From my arms, A picline
Feeder snaked out
Of my carotid artery, a
Feeder tube left, but no
Longer needed, in my neck

To my stomach, and one
Bulb-drain, one pigtail
Drain and one
Colostomy bag, bulged my
Shirt like so many plastic

Tumors. My face, once
Considered pleasing to
Look at, had become a
Deaths-head.
I've spoken of my weight

Dropping like a deflating
Balloon. I, then, resembled
One. Soft, flabby and
Formless. Excess stomach
Acid yellowed and rotted

My teeth, and left my
Perpetually swollen tongue
Burned and stinging. All
That could be mended,
Would be, within

Four to six years. Other
Aspects of my desiccation
Would never be.

PART THREE:
Out of the Pit

Canto XI- First Steps

There are some roads
Which, having left their
Wearisome length, we
Remember each dark,
Dreary step forever.

Trudging in creeping slow
Return to, hopefully, once
Again sit steady, calm in
Acceptance of life's
Rightful luxuries, work,

Food, thinking, feeling and
Energized independence,
My motivation was fueled,
Syrup-slow, by willpower
And an opaque belief that I

Would shake loose of
Pain's chains, and be free
Of sloth and agony. I had
Mended through lesser
Hurts past- broken bones,

Bruises and strained
Muscles. So, it was never
An anchor to my spirit or

Mind, nor was it ever
Suggested, that I would

End my life in the abyss.
Carrying an ever-lit lantern
Of need, I went where
Necessity directed
Me, and accomplished

Daily survival because I
Knew no other way. A
Mountain of medication sat
Atop my options; forcing
Myself to eat and sleep.

And, eventually, to find the
Wherewithal to work.
Following five weeks of
Radiation therapy, cringing
Beneath yet another

Machine suspended like
Damocles' blade over my
Shivering self, (I made the
Somber decision to forego
Chemotherapy

In a Quality-of-life-
Decision, should my
Recovery from the
Whipple surgery prove
Futile), I took the drastic

Forward-thinking step of
Embarking on a week-long
Cruise to the Western
Caribbean. Past cruises
Leant me the false belief I

Could ignore my Abysmal
Journey, and dance, drink
And gamble once again. I
Would see new sights and
Meet new people. I

Reasoned this to
Be a needed distraction
From the thick, red
Discomfort I was
Experiencing. I let hope

And a blind, stumbling
Optimism delude me. In
Most aspects, this trip
Proved to
Be a mistake. Although it

Ended up as a turning point
In my recovery efforts, a
Distinct and colorful
Reminder that life was
Continuing on in the

World,
Regardless of my
Difficulties, and that my

Own sense of self-
Importance did not see the

World suffering as I did, I
Was too exhausted and
Covered in emotional
Calluses to fully enjoy and
Appreciate my day-trip to

The Aztec ruins I had
Wanted to see for years.
Relaxing on the
Deck of the ship was a
Leaden weight on my

Shoulders, as I saw others
Enjoying the sunny days
And evening activities
I could only watch. The
Scenery was fresh and

Wonderful. The pain and
Nausea were persistent and
Difficult. Recovery is slow
When
All is appreciated only by

My eyes, and not by my
Heart and feelings. Then,
Back to the job and the
Understanding and patient
People I worked with. I

Considered myself
Fortunate if I could
Complete a four-hour
Stretch in a day, my head
An anchor weight bent

Over my already bruised
And bowed shoulders, and
Recall
Even a small portion of the
Details the job required.

But, to my way of
Thinking, such as it was, I
Had resumed my former
Life. All would be well,
Eventually, the ghost of
My hope assured me.

Prophetically, this turned
Out to be true.

Canto XII– Bleeding Begins

The tide of my energy was
Already ebbing my care
And concern out to the sea
Of disquiet. My unfocused
Attention, sliding like mud

From one half-understood
Customer to another, made
Work a worrisome task,
My abilities not up to my
Usual standards. Then,

Approximately four
Months after returning to
The job, something new to
My fretful travail arose. I
Was plagued by a growing

Headache, and my heart
Struggled with simple
Tasks, like climbing stairs.

Then, one day, calamity
Struck.

A trip to the
Bathroom. I sit; I finish.
Upon standing, I see a
Sight that will become
Familiar to me for years,

Possibly, the rest of my
Life. There is a deep, red
Tint in the bowl!
Bloody noses in the past
Suggested what it was I

Was losing. Blood-red and
Frightening, I didn't panic,
Because panic was a
Reaction I was unfamiliar
With. The slow, slogging

Marsh that my brain had
Become
Didn't process the need for
Action for two more days,
When I was shaking and

Unsteady. I drove to an
Urgent care facility, to be
Told I needed four units of
Blood at a hospital. And so
Started the scopes and

Scans to find the cause. So
Unfamiliar were my
doctor-
Knights with the state my
Cancer removal had left

Me in, that it took six years
Of wrong turnings and

Misleads, and
Approximately thirty-six
Units of transfused blood,

To find the cause.
An enlarged spleen,
Rupturing at a small,
Insignificant artery, and
Emptying itself, was the

End result. As my white-
Count increased, at a
Snail's pace, this would
Become less of a problem,
Occurring only three to

Four times a year, then
Less. But,
At first, with my anemia in
Full force, the blood loss
Meant monthly trips to the

Emergency room. I took it
In stride. It had proven to
Be treatable with
Transfusions. But, in the
Absence of any whys or

Wherefores, it was terrible.
It was disgusting. It simply
Sucked.

Canto XIII- Beach's First Breeze

Two years after the
Whipple surgery, I made
The decision to go home.
Not the apartment I lived
In, my home of the past. I

Grew up in Huntington
Beach, California, a place
Of lighter, easier attitudes,
And with a reputation as a
Vacation spot. For me, it

Meant the memories of my
School days up to junior
College, including school
Theater productions,
Playing the drums in

Various bands and my first
Relationships. The old,
Tiny Main Street Library,
Where I enjoyed early
Summer reading programs,

Was, and
Still is, a favorite hiding
Place for my heart and
Memories. And these
Feelings, surprisingly,

Began to wend their way
Past my depression, to
Reconnect me with myself.
Some days, I sat on the
Pier and remembered

Fishing with my dad and
Brother. Others, I would
Breathe in the same
Stinging, salty air I had,
Decades before, enjoyed as

I girl-watched with my
High-school friend, Jeff. I
Felt a
Small sadness for the loss
Of the Golden Bear, a jazz

Spot on Pacific Coast
Highway, demolished
Years before. All these
Memories, enjoyed on
Many return trips,

Amazed and invigorated
Me. Amazing that I was
Feeling something.
Invigorating because this
All was me incarnate. My

Favorite high-school snack
Was something called
'strips and cheese', a
Precursor to, and superior
Version of, nachos.

Finding a restaurant that
Still made them as I
Remembered was an
Incredible and
Strengthening experience.

It occurred to me one day,
Munching on them, that I
Had survived, and was
Continuing to survive, my
Trek through the abyss.

One Saturday morning,
Walking through the
Outdoor hallways of the
High-school I had
Attended, and

Expecting to get asked to
Leave by campus police, I
Felt a warm nostalgia for
Those days, when I wasn't
Plagued by ill-health and

Responsibilities. And, I
Loved the feeling. Hell, I
Loved feeling again. And,

Even though I knew my
Dire circumstance was

Waiting in the wings,
Ready to show itself at any
Moment, I didn't care.
And, so far, it hasn't. I'm
Keeping alert, just in

Case. So, my days at the
Beach are back. What
Could be better?

Only one Thing…

CANTO XIV- Women Again

A landscape. Grateful to
Finally be able to
Appreciate and revisit,
After so long away,
Sojourning in fretful fear,

Far from feminine
Curves, scents, soft, silky,
Satin skin. Once again
Inhaling aromas of close-in
Seeing and hearing and

Smelling. Again listening
To a
Voice higher-pitched than
My own, chowing down on
Endearments which my

Family and friends can't
Whisper, and thrilled to
Answer in kind. Back to
The beach, and beautiful
Bikini-clad, running,

Volleyball bouncing net
Slams; soaked surfing sea
Drenched wet;
Lazy towel lying, bronzed
And burning, basted in

Protective oil, a feast for
My eyes, my heart, my
Spirit. Dinners looking into
Laughing eyes
And carefree smiles,

Thrilling once more with
The possibilities, for the
Night or for life. Signals
Sent out in hopeful
Anticipation, sturdy

Against 'denied', but still
Admitting to my myself
That persistence, charm
And honesty will prevail in
A reward of deeper

Meaning
And payoff- a memory.
The occasional hug, warm
And welcome, and
Pleasing distant from the

Old days of 'How many
Notches did I get
This year?', matches of
Macho, empty bragging
And lies about laying,

Now, a true Taste. A
heaven

Of lips against mine, only
For a moment, of imbibing

A puff of breath laced with
An airy leftover from what
She had for dinner, a
Quickly
Paralyzing push of softly

Yielding mounds, mashed
Laughing and long in
Answer to a two-way tune
Of "Maybe next time."
Still, a victory.

My heroine of tongue and
Hair and earlobes, jeans
And heels and handbag,
Holding me just long
Enough to prove my recent

Years of discomfort
And unhealth have not left
Me permanently bereft,
Holding me just long
Enough to prove that

Everything still works as it
Should. I can't
Read enough description
About women and their
Delights. My focus, no

Longer nailed to my pain,
Being now on many things,
Among the
Most pleasant, those jewels
Of distraction- makeup,

Perfume and panties. Hip-
Swaying, sauntering walks
And endless poses of
'Look at me!'
Absolutely wonderful.

And, every one of these
Momentary Aphrodites
Exhibit the absolutely
Unique. Not just for me,
But, just for

Me. And one another.
Outdoing each other in a
Grab of attention, not just
From me, but all eyes
Interested in a grateful

Gaze of give-me-
Your-attention, your
Longing, your long. And,
My role in this contest, as a
Man vying for the brass

Ring, this contest of 'Keep
Trying, the chase is

Half the fun,' sees me
Sending my missives of
Hope away to be analyzed

And judged and given the
'thumbs up' or 'thumbs
down', knowing that
Sometimes the anticipation
Has to be enough. What's

It cost, after all? The price
Of a dinner? Completely
Worth it.

Canto XV- What's Left to Describe?

And so. My life moves and
Shifts and continues as it
Should. I've always
Appreciated life in all its
Forms, colors and flavors.

Now, I have the means for
Expressing that
Appreciation. What about
Tomorrow? Who knows?
Who cares? I plan for the

Morrow, but have to stay
Ready. We all do. We've
Always had to be on the
Lookout with regards our
Health. All of us face a

Certain ending. And that
Ending is always too soon.
Just remember, some of us
Have trekked the abyss.
Some still do. Just spare us

A thought, then go on.
You're what life's all
About.

Be safe.

CANTO XVI- Forward Thoughts, Forward Feelings

Sun Sol Breeze

A mouth-filling freshest
breeze.
Clear coolness of kite
flying
Kidhood rewind on a
Saturday today also
yesterday.

Zephyr whispers "My
love"
To me for staying and
Replying in kind. Nothing
Of the recent darkness
today;
Only post-rain perfection
of
Reaffirmation in this
Spinning bio-sphere.

'Clean' is the word and
way of
This breathing, blowing
Clouderpuff pushing past.
'Grateful'
Is the fated way I face the
Soft warmth of Sol Star's
tepid

Temperance of the
delicious
Windy treat.
Temperate cool- perfection
in action.

Recouping Vacation

My job done, my nine to
five.
Long hours made longer by
draining, impactful health
harm. I'm speaking post-
cancer surgery. Red stress

and black depress made
doctors say "Time to
redress". Slogging in
habitual muck of languor
and morale pitched low,
'Quality of life'

is the sawbones motto.
Emotional, mental,
physical, it's all one. Years
of a painful remind that my
pancreas was almost my
surcease,

have left me bereft of
motivation towards
movement. My locus of
focus-my torso; Whipple
surgery, my life-save, my
'C'- stave. But, not enough
recoup time did I allow
myself. Always 'Back to
work'. For most, lay-off is

a one-off to worry, fear,
dread. For me,

time to rest, write and
rejuvenate. Pursue this new
avenue for expressing
feelings felt with disasters
dealt with.

Not a bad start.

The Beach Near Home

How do I avoid the clichés
of description? The deep-
felt thud of water power
fueled by a pushing,
pulling gravity,

crowning white wakes of
endless unconcern for the
wading, swimming,
surfing, splashing co-
minglers,

relaxing and reflecting on
nothing or everything as
cares evaporate with the
twisting, misted waves as I

watch in excitement of
memories from the lighter
times of school, escape,
adventure, lightening my

weighted shoulders and
connecting me, long-stride,
with relief that my days
done are not gone, just
covered in hazy
obscuration by the
churning

rapids of water under a
bridge. How do I strip
away the platitudes of non-

description, to lay bare my
heart, as one who smells
the ocean breeze,

cool, calming and acrid?
Salty, stinging, tasting
without eating the fish
therein, toothsome, sweet
savor of a hundred baited
hooks cast

pier-side, to later gut and
scale and grill in a sizzling,
popping sensation for my
ears and waiting tongue

buds. It returns to me in a
flash of smiling movie
memories, an angel-wing
assurance saying 'Don't
worry, love, you're not far
from home'.

The Bowl Is Red

Once again, a rose of color,
Shocking in its sudden
seeing,

Knowing my warmth and
life's food, sustenance, is
bleeding away in a
headache

of pressure dropped. But,
not too fearful, as the trek
marches on, through

marshes, slogged through
before, all in stride, to
watch in fascinated dread,
no panic

for life's great fuel gone.
Then, bone morrow
working in wondrous ways
to fill

again my spill and color
my pallor to pink, skin
color fading in a
translucent

parody of nature's
intention, then slow-filling

back to where I wear a skin
as meant

by life and love and peace
of mind. For a time,
anyway.

The March

All in front of me. My gaze
rich in deep colored
tapestry of every possible
hue gain and going in the
world. All was my
education, nothing

was forsaken. No
judgments about anything.
Every day is decision about
which treasure to find and
love. All is wealth; friends,
family,

school, play. Silent mind
staring and sharing and
slowly knowing more and
more to store it all in my
sponge-attic. Light was

welcome. Friends were a
fun-filled joke to share
with. Then, there were
girls, a softer, sleeker, satin
better half to my ridiculous

clumsiness. Years of life
expanded me, 'til I felt full
and important. I was. We
all are.

That was then.

Now is middle age.
Deflated and shrunken by
trying to move mountains
and then almost being
crushed by one. My
mountain in metaphor-

Cancer of the pancreatic
kind. No more seeing a
place in the world of
worthiness. Now, only
living three-quarters within
myself to

hold onto the meaning,
never gone, just buried
beneath a current of
discomfort. Better than the
alternative, for sure. But,
I've

definitely become high-
maintenance. There is
more comfort in the dark.
Light is a call to action and
activity, not as easy as it
used to be. Dark

means cool rest at the end
of a hard day, even during
the day. No doubt, a deeper

meaning than that, so
Freud would probably say.
It

doesn't matter. My heart
beats, my eyes see, my ears
hear and I still dream,
asleep and awake . What
else is there; should there
be?

This is now.

Park.1

Cool light blue calm silver
mist. Sanded, planed
eroded bench, shirt-
waving, gentle zephyr.
Excited, free children
screaming just to scream,
to hear themselves. A
distant plane propeller
buzz accentuates the quiet,
punctuates the warm calm;
noisy life is far away.
Yellow-white sunlight
bright reflecting back sand-
brown down beneath my
chuck-clad clod-hoppers.
Coal color shadows, some
light-blue-gray move to
different wind motives,
sway to their own
shadowed self-importance.

A car horn
Fading
Doppler affect

Zephyr breath
Beach breeze
This is summer?

Ocean Air
Drum sticks
Branches moving

Sitting calmly still
Does it fill or empty me?
My shadow shirt moves

Park.2

The sun on my notepad.
Lighter, dimmer. Because
of the trees behind me, or
clouds passing? Dogs,
three precisely, straining at
their leash, not
understanding their place
in the world, still chasing
the squirrel, their dog-mind
Consumed. Never seen a
squirrel stationary and still
alive. The magic of this
park. Trees as tall now as
when I walked here young.
Probably not.
Proportionate. Both of us
sprouts. That's a tiny
lizard.

Breathe that warm, deep
air
Eucalyptus trees in bloom
Thick and glorious

Burn my tongue
Cool off
Let it sit, man

Provolone
Cheesy
It's metaphor

Waves in thick
Odor
Kitchen magic

Park.3

Man-made lake, the same
seven-foot log in its dried-
up center. Over-grown and
useless, except to
dragonflies and kite flyers.
Leafy compost stirs the
cycle from then to now.
Yellow-green blue budded
bushes line a lively lane of
ladies and gentlemen going
gone, both walking and
living. A leaf blower
barking. Just part of the
scenery.

Sleepy Timey

Tension fading, muscles
deflating balloon shrink
comfort. Eyelids covering
red-veined blue, green,
brown orbs, light strobes,
rods throwing dimmer,
dimmer hoping to dream
strong, sweet better
tomorrows. Adventure.
Action in stillness. Truth in
action, some say. Healing
story telling. Starry time.
Or, blank blanket psych
void. Temporary bye-bye
time to issues, problems.
Motor boat dialog.

www.ingramcontent.com/pod-product-compliance
Lightning Source LLC
LaVergne TN
LVHW011213080426
835508LV00007B/753